扫描文章前的二维码
收听该故事的英文音频

"伟人的少年故事"丛书

奇妙的物理学

推动物理学变革的惊世奇才

(斯里兰卡)努雷·维塔奇(Nury Vittachi) 著
斯泰帕·张(Step Cheung) 图
朱之翀 译　张群 审校

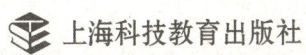

图书在版编目(CIP)数据

奇妙的物理学：推动物理学变革的惊世奇才/(斯里)努雷·维塔奇(Nury Vittachi)著；朱之翀译.—上海：上海科技教育出版社，2018.8

("伟人的少年故事"丛书)

书名原文：Fabulous Physics

ISBN 978-7-5428-6710-0

I.①奇… II.①努… ②朱… III.①物理学家—生平事迹—世界—青少年读物 IV.① K816.1—49

中国版本图书馆CIP数据核字(2018)第069150号

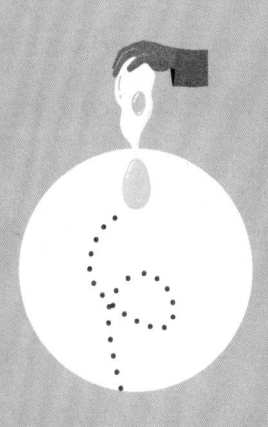

Contents

Wilhelm Rontgen The Man Who Saw a Living Skeleton   3

Marie Curie The Servant Girl Who Beat Einstein   10

Abdus Salam The Boy Who Climbed to the Top   18

Wu Chien-Shiung The Quiet Queen of Physics   27

Michael Faraday The Boy Who Secretly Read the Books He Was Binding   34

Max Planck The Boy Who Didn't Listen to His Teacher   43

Albert Einstein How a Compass Inspired a Genius   51

Wolfgang Pauli The Boy Secretly Reading a Book Behind His School Desk   58

T.D. Lee The Student Whose Schools Kept Closing   66

John Von Neumann The Boy Who Had a Dispute with His Father   75

目 录

威廉·伦琴　看见了活人骨骼的男子　3

玛丽·居里　超越了爱因斯坦的女仆　10

阿卜杜勒·萨拉姆　登上科学高峰的男孩　18

吴健雄　文静的物理学女王　27

迈克尔·法拉第　在订书时悄悄读书的男孩　34

马克斯·普朗克　不听老师话的男孩　43

阿尔伯特·爱因斯坦　受到指南针启发的天才　51

沃尔夫冈·泡利　在课桌下偷偷看书的男孩　58

李政道　学业一再中断的学生　66

约翰·冯·诺伊曼　与父亲争论的男孩　75

THE MAN WHO SAW A LIVING SKELETON

威廉·伦琴
看见了活人骨骼的男子

WILHELM RONTGEN WAS A QUIET MAN, teaching science at a university.

But there was one thing special about him — he had a lot of **patience**①, and would try and try again to achieve what he wanted to achieve, never giving up.

※※※

When he had been a teenage boy in Germany in 1865, he wanted to go to university but did not have the right **qualifications**②. So instead, he got into a **polytechnic**③ when he was 19, and studied really hard.

Young Wilhelm was a patient person, and would try and try again, however long it took, to achieve what he wanted to achieve.

This was a good way to be. He did so well that 10 years later he was a professor at a university himself.

※※※

After that, every year was the same. He gave lectures for part of the week and did experiments for part of the week, because he wanted to make his own scientific discovery, not just spend his life teaching people about the findings of other scientists.

He did this right through his 30s, and then right through his 40s.

But he discovered nothing new.

By the time he was 50 years old, most people in his position would have stopped being **ambitious**④. They would have been happy enough to be old professors, ready for retirement.

威廉·伦琴（Wilhelm Rontgen）生性安静，他在一所大学里教科学。

不过，他的性格有一个特殊之处——特别有耐心，他会一遍遍地努力尝试，直到得出自己想要的结果，否则决不放弃。

1865 年，伦琴还是德国的一名少年，这时他就想上大学，但不够资格。19 岁时他去了一所专科学校，在那里刻苦学习。

年轻的威廉非常有耐心，自己想要得到的东西，他会一遍遍地尝试，无论这个过程需要多久。

这是个好习惯。他做得非常出色，因此在 10 年后，他成了一名大学教授。

从此以后，他的生活千篇一律，没有变化：每周花几天时间讲课，在剩下的几天里做实验。然而他想取得属于自己的科学发现，他不愿意把一生的时间都用于向人们传授其他科学家的发现上。

伦琴 30 多岁时这样做，40 多岁时也这样做。

但他并没有取得新的发现。

伦琴 50 岁了，大多数到他这个年龄的人都不再胸怀壮志，而是满足于做一名年长的教授，等待着退休。

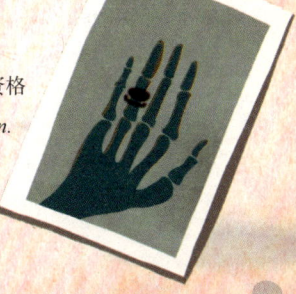

① **patience** [ˈpeɪʃ(ə)ns] *n.* 耐性、耐心，忍耐，容忍
② **qualification** [ˌkwɒlɪfɪˈkeɪʃ(ə)n] *n.* 资格、条件，限制，赋予资格
③ **polytechnic** [ˌpɒlɪˈteknɪk] *adj.* 各种工艺的、综合技术的；*n.* 工艺学校、理工专科学校
④ **ambitious** [æmˈbɪʃəs]; *adj.* 野心勃勃的、有雄心的，热望的，炫耀的 [more ambitious, most ambitious]

But not Wilhelm Rontgen. He kept doing experiments, never giving up.

One night, he was experimenting with vacuum tubes, which are glass **tubes**① filled with **electrified**② gas.

When he turned the lights off to see if the tube was glowing, he noticed a light shining on a work bench away from the desk. How odd!

He switched his experimental tube on and off a few times, but could still see something **glowing**③ on the bench.

In the dark, he lit a match to provide light, and walked over to the bench. A piece of cardboard with a chemical on it was glowing.

Rontgen realized that invisible rays were coming out of the tubes and crossing the room, somehow causing this chemical to glow.

He started doing experiments with these unknown rays, which he called X-rays, and learned strange things about them: they seemed to be able to go through solid surfaces. They could go through glass, or wood — or even skin.

Excited, he ate and slept in his laboratory so that he could do more experiments and learn more about these **mysterious**④ rays.

One day soon afterwards, he asked his wife Anna to hold up her hand, and he took a picture of it using X-rays. The picture showed a skeleton hand!

但是，威廉·伦琴不是这种人，他继续着实验，绝不言弃。

❦

一天晚上，伦琴用充满了带电气体的真空玻璃管做实验。

当他关上灯，想观察真空管是否发光时，他注意到离桌子很远的工作台上有亮光。真奇怪！

他多次反复地开关实验用的真空管，但仍能看到工作台上的某个东西在发光。

黑暗中他划着了一根火柴照明，然后向工作台走去。他发现卡纸上的一件化学品正在发光。

伦琴意识到，真空管放出了肉眼不可见的射线，射线穿过这间屋子，以某种方式引起了化学品发光。

他开始用这种不知名的射线做实验，并称其为 X 射线。他发现，这种射线具备一种奇怪的特性：似乎能够穿透固体表面。它能够穿透玻璃、木材——甚至皮肤。

伦琴非常激动，为了便于继续开展更多的实验，深入了解这种神秘的射线，他就在实验室吃饭、睡觉！

❦

不久后的一天，他让妻子安娜举起手，然后用 X 射线给这只手拍了一张照片。这张照片显示了一只看得见骨骼的手！

---

① **tube** ［tju:b］ *n.* 管、电子管、隧道、电视机；*vt.* 使成管状、把……装管、用管输送［tubed, tubed, tubing］

② **electrify** ［ɪˈlektrɪfaɪ］ *vt.* 使电气化、使充电、使触电、使激动［electrified, electrified, electrifying］

③ **glow** ［gləʊ］ *vi.* 发热、洋溢、绚丽夺目；*n.* 灼热、色彩鲜艳、兴高采烈

④ **mysterious** ［mɪˈstɪərɪəs］ *adj.* 神秘的、不可思议的

Anna gasped: "I have seen my own death!"

When Rontgen's discovery was shown to the world, he became famous. He was given the very first **Nobel Prize**[1] in Physics.

Today, machines based around his discovery of X-rays are used on most people at some time in their lives. Doctors use them to save the lives of patients.

And he also inspired Marie Curie, who we will meet in the next story.

But maybe Wilhelm Rontgen should really be remembered for his patience — the man who would never give up!

安娜震惊得喘不过气来："我看到了自己的死亡！"

当这个发现公之于世后，伦琴一下子声名鹊起。他被授予第一届诺贝尔物理学奖。

如今，大多数人在一生中，都曾经使用过基于伦琴发现的X射线所制造的机器。医生们用这种机器挽救了众多病人的生命。

伦琴的发现也启发了玛丽·居里，我们在下一个故事里会谈到她。

伦琴真正应该被人们所铭记的是他的耐心——这是一位永不言弃的男子！

---

① **Nobel Prizes** 诺贝尔奖，是以瑞典著名的化学家、硝化甘油炸药的发明人诺贝尔的部分遗产作为基金在1900年创立的。诺贝尔奖分设物理学、化学、生理学／医学、文学、和平和经济学六个奖项。在世界范围内，诺贝尔奖通常被认为是所颁奖的领域内最重要的奖项

THE SERVANT GIRL WHO BEAT EINSTEIN

玛丽·居里
超越了爱因斯坦的女仆

THE POOR YOUNG WOMAN who worked as a **domestic**[①] helper looking after children on a farm seemed destined to achieve nothing special in her life.

She was in her early 20s, but had already suffered a hard life.

Maria Sklodowska's mother had died when she was just 10 years old.

And her father was a science teacher who lost his job when he went on a **protest**[②] **calling for**[③] his small country, Poland, to be independent. It was governed at the time by Russia, a much bigger country.

Maria's dad was too poor to pay for education for his children but he gave them the one thing he had: a love of science.

The two girls in the family came up with a plan. The younger one would earn money working as a domestic helper looking after children, and the older one would study.

Then two years later, the older one, who hopefully would have a job and an income by then, would help the younger one, who could then study.

And so young Maria ended up looking after the children of a farmer.

The sisters' plan worked, keeping them both happy and occupied.

Two years later, Maria left the farm and went to Paris to study science, remembering the **marvelous**[④] things that her father had taught her. She changed her name **slightly**[⑤] to Marie, which sounded more French.

一位贫穷的年轻女子在一家农场当女仆,帮助照料那里的一群孩子。她的一生似乎注定碌碌无为。

她只有20岁出头,却已经经历了许多艰难困苦。

玛丽亚·斯科罗多夫斯卡(Maria Sklodowska)10岁时,母亲就去世了。

她的父亲曾经是一位科学教师,然而在参加了一次为祖国波兰争取独立的游行后,他就失业了。当时波兰是一个小国,被大国俄罗斯统治着。

玛丽亚的父亲失业后,没钱再送孩子们上学读书,但他送给了孩子们一件他所拥有的东西:对科学的热爱。

家中的两个女孩想出了一个办法:妹妹出去工作,给人家当女仆照料孩子,这样姐姐就有钱读书了。

两年后,姐姐就有希望找到一份工作,获得一定的收入。这样她就能够供妹妹去读书了。

这样,妹妹玛丽亚就不用再为农场主看管孩子了。

这对姐妹的计划生效了,她们俩忙碌而快乐着。

两年后,玛丽亚牢记着父亲的谆谆教诲,离开农场去巴黎研习科学。为了让名字听起来更具有法国味,她将自己原来的名字稍作改动,变成了玛丽(Marie)。

---

① **domestic** [dəˈmestɪk] *adj.* 国内的、家庭的,驯养的
② **protest** [prəˈtest; ˈprəʊtest] *vi.* 抗议、断言;*vt.* 抗议、断言;*n.* 抗议
③ **call for** 要求、需要、提倡、邀请、为……叫喊
④ **marvelous** [ˈmɑːvələs] *adj.* 了不起的、非凡的、令人惊异的、不平常的 [more marvelous, most marvelous]
⑤ **slightly** [ˈslaɪtlɪ] *adv.* 些微地、轻微地

One day, she went to visit a laboratory-for-hire because she needed a place to do her experiments — and met a handsome bearded Frenchman, who was the boss of the lab.

This man, Pierre Curie, fell in love with her, and they soon got married.

Her name was now Marie Curie. She read a science journal which said that a scientist named Wilhelm Rontgen (who we met in the previous story) had found amazing invisible rays coming out of a certain type of rock. He called them X-rays.

Invisible rays! What on earth could they be?

She decided that she would work out what they were, and find out if other substances gave out invisible rays.

For months, she and her husband worked on the challenge.

They **arranged for**① a cart pulled by a horse to bring a huge variety of substances to their lab so they could be tested to see if they gave out invisible rays.

Two great achievements followed. First, she discovered a substance, **radium**②, which gave out more invisible rays than had ever been measured before. And second, she thought of a good name for this new area of science: "**radioactivity**③".

❦❦❦

一天,她去参观一所对外出租的实验室,因为她需要一个做实验的地方。在那里,她遇到了实验室的老板,一位英俊的留着络腮胡的法国男子。

这位男子名叫皮埃尔·居里(Pierre Curie),他与玛丽坠入了爱河,两人很快就结婚了。

玛丽现在叫玛丽·居里(Marie Curie)了。她阅读一本科学杂志时了解到,一位名叫威廉·伦琴(我们在上一个故事中提到了他)的科学家发现了一种神奇的由特定岩石发出的不可见射线,他将其命名为X射线。

肉眼看不到的射线!这究竟是什么?她决定查明其中的真相,探究是否存在其他能够发出不可见射线的物质。

她和丈夫针对这个难题研究了好几个月。

他们安排了一辆马车,运输大量不同的物质到实验室,在那里测试这些物质能否发出不可见射线。

❦❦❦

他们取得了两项成就。第一项是,玛丽发现了一种叫作镭的物质,它发出的不可见射线比任何其他测试过的物质都要多。第二项是,玛丽为这一新兴的科学领域想出了一个恰当的名字:"放射性"。

---

① **arrange for** 安排、为……做准备
② **radium** [ˈreɪdɪəm] *n.* 镭(88号元素符号Ra)
③ **radioactivity** [ˌreɪdɪəʊækˈtɪvɪtɪ] *n.* 放射性、放射能力、放射现象

Invisible rays had a lot of practical uses, especially in detecting broken bones.

Years later, Marie and her daughter organized X-ray units to be taken out to the places where soldiers were fighting in World War I and they saved many lives. They also discovered that radiation could be used to kill the disease called **cancer**[①].

Marie was given TWO Nobel Prizes, and became friends with Einstein.

But one thing they didn't know in those days was that if a person spent a lot of time near radioactive machines it would make that person sick.

She died in 1934, aged 66, probably from having spent so much time near X-ray machines.

But she remains the most famous female scientist in history — not bad for a girl whose first job was working as a domestic helper for the children of a farmer.

肉眼不可见的射线有许多实用的功能,尤其在探测人体内的骨头是否受伤等方面。

很多年后,在第一次世界大战时,玛丽和她的女儿将 X 射线设备运到战场上,拯救了许多人的生命。她们也发现,可以利用辐射治疗癌症。

玛丽两次被授予诺贝尔奖,并和爱因斯坦成了好朋友。

但当时他们不知道的是,如果一个人长期接近放射性仪器,他/她会因辐射而患病。

玛丽于 1934 年去世,享年 66 岁。她的死因很可能是长期近距离接触 X 射线仪器。

尽管如此,玛丽仍然成了历史上最著名的女性科学家——对于第一份工作是照顾农场主孩子的女孩来说,这样的成就很了不起。

① **cancer** [ˈkænsə] *n.* 癌症、恶性肿瘤

THE BOY WHO CLIMBED TO THE TOP

阿卜杜勒·萨拉姆
登上科学高峰的男孩

A LONG TIME AGO, a man living in India had a dream. He saw his tiny son, Abdus Salam, climbing a tree.

"Be careful," the worried father called out.

The little boy, hardly pausing on his upward journey, shouted down: "Don't worry, Dad. I know what I'm doing."

The small child climbed higher and higher, and eventually clambered right **out of sight**[①], lost in the clouds.

The dream ended. The man woke up and went to give his sleeping child a kiss.

Little Abdus Salam was a very smart child, and at a young age was reading books in different languages and doing mathematics for fun. He lived in a very poor part of India called Jhang, which is now in Pakistan. His parents valued education and encouraged him to continue to learn.

When the boy reached the age of 14, he sat for the university entrance exam and managed to get in.

The boy's father was very proud. He believed that his son could do anything. But what should his job be, after he graduated while still a **teenager**[②]? In those days, the 1940s, the highest achievement the dad could think of was for his son to get a job working for the then Indian Railways.

But things did not go well. For a start, the boy had spent a lot of time staying up late at night reading, which meant that he wore glasses — so his eyesight was considered a problem. Then they discovered that there were rules about how old you had to be to join the railways, and Abdus Salam was too young.

很久以前,一个印度男子做了一个梦:他梦见年幼的儿子阿卜杜斯·萨拉姆(Abdus Salam)在爬一棵树。

"注意安全,"父亲担忧地提醒儿子。

儿子向上攀爬的动作几乎没有一丝停顿,他对父亲喊道:"别担心,爸爸,我知道自己在做什么。"

小男孩爬得越来越高,最终爬上了云端,消失在父亲的视野之外。梦就这样结束了。男子醒来,亲了亲睡梦中的儿子。

✦✦✦

小萨拉姆很聪明,还在很小的年纪时,他就把阅读不同语言的书籍和做数学运算当作消遣娱乐。他住在印度章县,那是一个非常贫穷的地方,现在属于巴基斯坦。他的父母很重视教育,鼓励他不断学习。

在 14 岁时,萨拉姆参加了大学入学考试并且胜利通过。

他的父亲非常自豪,他相信,以儿子的能力,做任何事都不在话下。但是儿子毕业时还是个少年,能做什么工作呢?当时是 20 世纪 40 年代,在这位父亲的观念中,儿子能达到的最高成就,就是毕业后在印度铁路局觅得一份工作。

但是事不遂人愿。首先,萨拉姆常常熬夜看书,导致他不得不戴上眼镜——他的近视成了一个大问题;接着,他们发现进入铁路局是有年龄限制的,而阿卜杜斯·萨拉姆年龄太小了。

---

① **out of sight** 看不见、在视野之外、在看不见的地方
② **teenager** [ˈtiːneɪdʒə] n. 十几岁的青少年、13 岁到 19 岁的少年

So his **brilliance**[①] had made him a failure.

Life was so unfair!

Disappointed, the boy went back to university to do what he knew he could do: studying books. It turned out to be the right move. He managed to win a **scholarship**[②] to study at another university — Cambridge in the UK.

Have you heard of Cambridge? It's one of world's top universities. Abdus Salam travelled to the UK and found that he fitted like a **glove**[③] among the thinkers at the university city.

He became a top scientist, although he kept his love of Asian culture. When he met Albert Einstein, Abdus Salam talked to him about eastern views of God and religion, and Einstein was fascinated, finding interesting **parallels**[④] between what he heard and what was being discussed by the **quantum physics**[⑤] community.

Back in India, the boy's father missed his son, of course, but he soon saw Abdus Salam's face again. It was in newspapers around the world when the boy from a poor part of Pakistan won the Nobel Prize.

The dad also realized that the dream that he had had many years before had come true, in a metaphorical way.

所以，他的才华反而导致了他的失败。

命运真不公平啊！

<hr />

萨拉姆失望地回到大学，去做他认为自己可以做的事——看书。这最终被认为是一项正确的举措。萨拉姆成功申请到一笔奖学金，可以去另一所大学——英国的剑桥大学学习。

你听说过剑桥大学吗？那是世界上最顶尖的大学之一。阿卜杜勒·萨拉姆到达英国后，发现自己身处大学城的思想家之间，简直如鱼得水。

萨拉姆成了一名顶尖的科学家，尽管他仍然喜爱着亚洲文化。当他与爱因斯坦相遇时，他向爱因斯坦谈起东方人对上帝和宗教的看法，爱因斯坦对此很着迷，发现萨拉姆向他讲述的和量子物理学科学家们所讨论的两者之间存在着有趣的相似之处。

<hr />

萨拉姆远在印度的父亲当然很想念自己的儿子，不过他很快就再次见到了儿子的容貌。萨拉姆的照片被印在了全世界的报纸上。因为他——一位来自巴基斯坦贫穷地区的男孩，获得了诺贝尔奖。

这位父亲突然意识到，自己多年前的那个梦境，以一种隐喻性的方式实现了。

---

① **brilliance** [ˈbrɪlj(ə)ns] *n.* 光辉、才华，宏伟
② **scholarship** [ˈskɒləʃɪp] *n.* 奖学金
③ **glove** [ɡlʌv] *n.* 手套、*vt.* 给……戴手套 [gloved , gloved , gloving]
④ **parallel** [ˈpærəlel] *n.* 平行线、对比；*vt.* 使……与……平行；*adj.* 平行的、类似的、相同的 [paralleled 或 -allelled , paralleled 或 -allelled , paralleling 或 -allelling]
⑤ **quantum physics** 量子物理学

His boy had climbed a tall tree, causing worries for his parents, and had eventually climbed right out of sight.

And he remembered the child's words in the dream: "Don't worry, Dad. I know what I'm doing."

萨拉姆爬上了一棵大树，尽管父母对此忧心忡忡，他最终达到了常人所不能企及的高度。

这位父亲一直记得梦中萨拉姆说的那句话："别担心，爸爸，我知道自己在做什么。"

THE QUIET QUEEN OF PHYSICS

吴健雄
文静的物理学女王

A TEENAGE GIRL HAD A PROBLEM. Her parents were among the few in China who believed that girls should be educated, and she had won a position in The Normal School — a place which was anything but normal. It was a famous boarding school near Shanghai, specializing in art and **literature** ①.

But the problem was this: the thing that the girl, Wu Chien-Shiung, really loved, was science, which was a Boy Subject. Girls were not allowed to study it.

So, after a full day at school, she would work in the evenings, as the stars came out, on books on physics and chemistry.

Still, there's nothing teachers love more than to see students who really want to learn — so they quietly encouraged her, and she eventually ended up studying physics at a university in China.

It may be that she worked harder than her classmates, to prove that women could study subjects men thought were too difficult for them.

Her professors told the ambitious, hardworking young woman that all the top work in physics in those days, the 1930s, was happening not in China, but in the West. So Wu Chien-Shiung got on a boat and sailed to the USA.

Even there, women scientists were rare. Still, she was hard-working and **reliable** ② and **willing** ③ to play a secondary role, staying in the background.

She did much of the experimental work for two male scientists, Lee Tsung-Dao and Yang Chen-Ning, who were given the Nobel Prize for the resulting discoveries.

一位年轻的姑娘遇到了一个问题。她的父母是中国为数不多的认为女孩也应该接受教育的父母，因此她进入了一所师范院校就读——这是一所很不寻常的学校。它靠近上海，是一所著名的寄宿制学校，精于艺术和文学。

　　问题在于：这位名叫吴健雄的小姑娘热爱的是科学，但在当时，科学是一门只有男性才被允许学习的学科，因此她不能攻读科学。

　　所以，当吴健雄在学校里上完了一整天的课程后，她只能在晚上，借着星光阅读物理学和化学方面的书籍。

❧❧❧

　　当然，老师们都很喜爱这种热衷于学习的学生——所以他们默默地在背后鼓励吴健雄，最终吴健雄在中国的一所大学里读完了物理学。

　　可能是为了证明女性也能够攻读那些男性认为对女性来说太困难的学科，在大学里，吴健雄学得比其他同学都更努力。

　　当时是 20 世纪 30 年代，吴健雄的教授们告诉这位胸怀大志、刻苦学习的年轻女子，中国的物理学高等教育不如西方，所以吴健雄乘船远赴美国。

　　即使在美国，女性科学家也为数不多。吴健雄仍然努力学习，她是一位可信赖的人，乐于在幕后扮演助手的角色。

　　她为两位男性科学家李振道和杨振宁做了许多实验，最后他俩因为取得的杰出的成就被授予了诺贝尔奖。

---

① **literature** ［ˈlɪt(ə)rətʃə］ *n.* 文学、文献，文艺，著作
② **reliable** ［rɪˈlaɪəb(ə)l］ *adj.* 可靠的、可信赖的［more reliable，most reliable］
③ **willing** ［ˈwɪlɪŋ］ *adj.* 乐意的、自愿的、心甘情愿的［more willing，most willing］

During World War II, she worked on a secret **assignment**[1] to create the first atom bomb, but that project is associated with famous male scientists.

In fact, her career can be summed up like this: "It's amazing what you can achieve if you don't mind who gets the **credit**[2]!"

There was one sad thing in her life: China went through a period of **upheaval**[3] and unrest from the war until the 1970s, and scientists were **blacklisted**[4] so she was not able to go back and visit her family often.

But she loved her work, and as the years went by, she became famous herself in the world of science. Some people called her "The First Lady of Physics", while others **addressed**[5] her as "Madame Wu". In 1975, she was elected the first female President of the American Physical Society.

When she died in 1997, her ashes were taken to be sprinkled at the primary school in China where she first studied.

  第二次世界大战期间，吴健雄和一些著名的男性科学家从事了一项秘密实验（指美国的原子弹研制项目"曼哈顿计划"），想要研制出第一颗原子弹。

  事实上，吴健雄的职业生涯可以这样概括："如果你不在乎谁最终获益，你就能取得惊人的成就！"

  但是在她的人生中，也有令人悲伤的事：20 世纪 70 年代，中国经历了一段动荡不安的岁月，因种种原因，吴健雄等科学家被列入黑名单，她不能经常回到故乡与家人团聚。

  她热爱自己的工作，随着时间的推移，她成为科学领域中的一位伟人。有人尊称她为"物理学第一夫人"，也有人称她为"吴夫人"。1975 年，她当选为美国物理学会第一任女会长。

  吴健雄于 1997 年去世，她的骨灰被送回中国，安葬在她曾经就读的小学（现为江苏省太仓市明德高级中学）里。

---

① **assignment** [ə'saɪnm(ə)nt] n. 分配、任务，作业、功课
② **credit** ['kredɪt] n. 信用、信誉、贷款、学分、信任、声望；vt. 相信、信任、把……归给、归功于
③ **upheaval** [ʌp'hiːv(ə)l] n. 剧变、隆起、举起
④ **blacklist** ['blæklɪst] n. 黑名单；vt. 将……列入黑名单
⑤ **address** [ə'dres] vt. 演说、写姓名地址、向……致辞、与……说话、提出、处理；n. 地址、演讲、致辞，说话的技巧，称呼

But before that, she'd become the first living scientist to have an **asteroid**① named after her. So, if you also like to read science books at night, like she did, look out of the window and point a telescope at the night sky.

Perhaps you might see a tiny light travelling past — one which bears the name 2752 Wu Chien-Shiung, named for the girl who studied late at night as the stars came out.

在此之前,她成为第一位在有生之年名字就被用于命名一颗小行星的科学家。所以,如果你像她一样,喜欢在晚上阅读科学类书籍,你可以望向窗外,用望远镜眺望星空。

说不定你能看到一颗星星——它的名字叫吴健雄,编号是 2752,以一个苦读至深夜群星闪耀时的女孩名字命名。

① **asteroid** [ˈæstərɔɪd] *n.* 小行星、海盘车、小游星;*adj.* 星状的

THE BOY WHO SECRETLY READ THE BOOKS HE WAS BINDING

迈克尔·法拉第
在订书时悄悄读书的男孩

A BOY AGED 14 HAD a mind full of questions — but nowhere to find answers. He came from a poor family in the UK, and they did not have enough money to send him to school, let alone university.

When they ran out of cash to buy food to eat, they told the boy, whose name was Michael Faraday, to go out to work to **learn a trade**[1] and earn money.

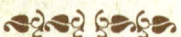

At the age of 14, he got a job for a man who hand-made books and ran a small bookshop.

This turned out to be a great place for Michael. He was **surrounded**[2] by knowledge, and could secretly read the books as he worked on **binding**[3] their pages together.

One of the books he read was about science — and he quickly fell in love with the subject. After that, he didn't just **skim**[4] the books, but taught himself science.

After he reached the age of 20, he started going to science lectures in London. This was the year 1812. At one of these, he made friends with a top scientist who was impressed by the attitude and knowledge of the young man who had not been to school or university.

一个 14 岁的男孩满脑子都是问题——但不知道在哪儿可以找到答案。他来自英国的一个贫困家庭，父母没钱供他上学读书，更不用说上大学了。

当家里所有的钱花光后，父母让这个名叫迈克尔·法拉第（Michael Faraday）的男孩去外面找工作，学一门手艺，赚钱养家。

法拉第 14 岁时，开始替一位手工制作书籍、同时经营着一家小书店的男子工作。

这家书店对于法拉第来说是一个极佳的地方，他沉浸在知识的海洋里。因为他的工作是把书页装订起来，所以他能够在订书的同时悄悄地读书。

他所阅读的书籍中，有一本是关于科学的——很快，他就爱上了这门学科。在那之后，他不再粗略地读这些书，而是认真地钻研起了科学。

1812 年，法拉第 20 岁，他开始去伦敦听有关科学的讲座。在一次讲座中，他与一位顶尖科学家交上了朋友。法拉第虽然没有上过学，却拥有极高的科学素养和渊博的知识，这给科学家留下了深刻印象。

① **learn a trade** 学一门手艺、学得一技之长
② **surround** [sə'raʊnd] vi. 被……环绕
③ **bind** [baɪnd] vi. 结合、装订，有约束力，过紧；vt. 绑、约束，装订，包扎，凝固 [bound, bound, binding]
④ **skim** [skɪm] vt. 略读、撇去……的浮物，从……表面飞掠而过、去除，（为逃税而）隐瞒（部分收入）；vi. 浏览、掠过 [skimmed, skimmed, skimming]

When the scientist's servant fell ill just before a trip, Michael was given the job.

But it was an unhappy time. The scientist's wife was one of those people who believed that servants and masters should be kept strictly separate, so poor Michael lived very **humbly**[1], had to sit outside the carriage even on cold, wet days, and had to eat separately from his boss. So there was no time for scientific discussions.

But eventually Michael did become an assistant scientist — and started making a huge number of discoveries himself.

He had a natural talent for it, and made finding after finding, becoming famous.

In fact, he eventually made so many scientific **breakthroughs**[2] that the other scientists wanted to make him president of the Royal Society, which was a club for the world's top scientists.

He refused. Because of his humble background, he said that he didn't want that sort of fame. Instead, he **volunteered**[3] for humble duties at the church to which he belonged.

In his lab, he discovered lots of things that no one had ever noticed before, particularly with regard to electricity and **magnetism**[4] and chemistry.

这位科学家的仆人恰巧在一次旅行前病倒了，法拉第因此得到了这一份工作。

但这并不是一次令人愉快的旅行。当时很多人认为，仆人和主人应该严格分开。这位科学家的妻子就持这样的观点。因此，可怜的法拉第居住环境非常简陋，即使是在寒冷潮湿的天气里，也不得不坐在马车外，也不能和主人一起用餐……这一切导致他们没有机会讨论科学。

❀❀❀❀❀

幸运的是，法拉第最后成了这位科学家的助理，并开始独立作出大量的科学发现。

他仿佛天生就具备这方面的才能，不断地作出新的科学发现，名气变得越来越大。

事实上，法拉第在科学方面取得了许多惊人的突破性进展，许多科学家都想让他担任世界上最顶尖的科学家俱乐部——英国皇家学会的会长。

但是法拉第拒绝了，他认为自己出身卑微，而且也不想沽名钓誉。他情愿为教堂尽一份绵薄之力。

在实验室中，法拉第发现了许多以前从来没有人注意到的新事物，尤其在电、磁和化学等方面。

---

① **humbly** ['hʌmbli] *adv.* 谦逊地、卑贱地、低声下气地
② **breakthrough** ['breɪkθruː] *n.* 突破、突破性进展
③ **volunteer** [ˌvɒlən'tɪə] *n.* 志愿者、志愿兵；*adj.* 志愿的；*vi.* 自愿；*vt.* 自愿
④ **magnetism** ['mæɡnɪtɪz(ə)m] *n.* 磁性、磁力、磁学，吸引力

Michael Faraday is much admired by scientists for the way he used his love of knowledge to get over the barriers of being poor and uneducated.

Maybe his greatest invention was finding a way to use electricity to create movement in machines. This was the **foundation**[1] of the electric motor.

Now if you think of all the objects around you that use electricity for power — cars, **vacuum cleaners**[2], electric toothbrushes, spaceships and almost every other device of technology — then you can see just how much he contributed.

Pretty amazing for a boy who only managed to get hold of books by sewing bindings on them!

Albert Einstein was stunned by how Michael Faraday combined a world-changing level of scientific genius with a gentle, **spiritual**[3] humbleness, and kept a picture of him in his study.

迈克尔·法拉第凭借着自己对知识的追求与热爱，克服了贫穷和没有受过教育的障碍，这一点得到了许多科学家的敬仰。

他作出的最伟大的一项发明，可能是找到了用电驱动机器运转的新方法，这成为电动机的理论基础。

如今，如果你想一想身边所有以电为动力的物体，比如汽车、吸尘器、电动牙刷、宇宙飞船以及其他几乎所有的科技设备，你就可以感受到，法拉第对社会作出了多么巨大的贡献！

对于一个只有在装订书籍的时候才有机会读书的男孩来说，这一切是多么令人惊奇啊！

法拉第是改变了世界的科学天才，但他性情温和，为人谦逊，连爱因斯坦也为之震惊，并在自己的书房中摆放了一张法拉第的画像。

① **foundation** [faʊnˈdeɪʃ(ə)n] *n.* 基础、地基，基金会，根据、创立
② **vacuum cleaner** [ˈvækjuəm ˈkliːnə] 吸尘器、真空吸尘器
③ **spiritual** [ˈspɪrɪtʃʊəl；-tjʊəl] *adj.* 精神的、心灵的。

THE BOY WHO DIDN'T LISTEN TO HIS TEACHER

马克斯·普朗克
不听老师话的男孩

STEP C.

A TEENAGE BOY HAD a problem. Like many students, Max had a favorite subject. But his teacher told him there was no future in his area of interest, which was physics. It was the late 1800s and scientists had found everything there was to be found.

"In this field, almost everything is already discovered, and all that remains is to fill a few holes," said his teacher Philipp von Jolly.

Boo! What a shame. Max Planck loved physics and felt that he would have loved to have gone on to be a scientist, discovering lots of important new things.

But what else could he do? Max was also very good at music — he could sing well, and play many different **instruments**①. So that was an **option**②.

Max was quite a spiritual boy, and in the end he decided to go with what he felt called to do in his heart: he chose to stay with physics, against the advice of his own science teacher.

He did well in his studies at university, and soon became a professor of physics — that "finished" line of investigation.

One day an electrical company asked Professor Planck to help them improve their light bulbs. This was the 1890s, and electric lights had become popular in Europe.

At that time, scientists were very puzzled about the nature of light, but could make no progress in their attempts to understand it better.

少年马克斯遇到了一个问题。同其他学生一样，他也有自己最喜欢的学科，但是老师告诉他，他喜欢的那门学科——物理学是没有未来的。当时是 19 世纪下半叶，所有该被发现的东西都已经被科学家发现了。

"在物理学方面，几乎没有什么未知的领域了，剩下要做的只是填补一些不重要的空白。"他的老师菲利普·冯·约利（Philipp von Jolly）这样对他说。

真是太遗憾了！马克斯·普朗克（Max Planck）深爱着物理学，甚至想要成为一名科学家，去发现与众不同的新事物。

但除了物理学，他还能做些什么呢？马克斯在音乐方面也很擅长——他歌唱得很好听，还会演奏好多种乐器。所以音乐也可以是他的一种选择。

马克斯是一位有精神追求的男孩，最终他决定遵从内心的抉择，继续物理学的研究，哪怕这个决定与他的科学老师的建议相悖。

在大学里，马克斯学习成绩优异，很快成为物理学——这门已经"完成"研究的学科的教授。

※※※※※※

有一天，一家电力公司请普朗克教授帮助他们改进电灯泡。当时是 19 世纪 90 年代，电灯在欧洲很流行。

那时的科学家们对于光的性质所知甚少，尽管他们努力进行探索研究，但收效甚微。

---

① **instrument** ['ɪnstrʊm(ə)nt] *n.* 仪器、工具、乐器、手段、器械
② **option** ['ɒpʃ(ə)n] *n.* 选项、选择权、买卖的特权

Max looked at how light worked and eventually had a **brainwave**[1]. Light energy comes in little tiny pieces, too small to see, he realized. He named the parts using the Latin word for piece, which is "quantum".

At that stage in history, most people thought light was a wave, so his idea was quite **revolutionary**[2].

Despite the simplicity of the idea, it turned out to be a notion that would turn science upside down.

That year, 1900, he was walking in the snow with one of his children, and he revealed that he had discovered something that might make him famous, like Isaac Newton. He was right.

Many other people, including Albert Einstein, one of the most famous scientists of all time, joined Planck in investigating this new discovery and the result was "quantum mechanics" — a new branch of study that soon became the **dominant**[3] part of physics.

One of the strangest discoveries was that **reality itself**[4] is made up of tiny individual pieces which have a minimum size, like **pixels**[5].

马克斯考虑着光的工作原理,突然灵光一闪。他意识到,光能是以肉眼不可见的一个一个非常微小的能量单位传递的。他用拉丁文中表示"小块"的单词将这种能量单位称为"量子"。

在那个历史时期,大多数人认为光是一种波,所以他的这个观点是革命性的发现。

这个观点并不复杂,但它最终给科学界带来了翻天覆地的变化。

1900年的一天,普朗克与他的一个孩子一起走在雪地里,突然意识到,他的这个发现可能会使他一举成名,成为和牛顿一样著名的人物。他的感觉是对的。

当时有很多人,包括有史以来最著名的一位科学家——爱因斯坦,都加入了普朗克这一新发现的研究队伍,他们的最终成果——创立"量子力学"——这一崭新的分支很快成为物理学的主流。

在他们得出的结论中,最令人惊讶的一个发现是:实体本身是由微小的块构成的,这些小块是最小尺寸的单体,就如同像素一样。

---

① **brainwave** ['brenwev] *n.* 脑电波、灵感
② **revolutionary** [revə'luːʃ(ə)n(ə)rɪ] *adj.* 革命的、大变革的,旋转的;*n.* 革命者 [revolutionaries]
③ **dominant** ['dɒmɪnənt] *adj.* 显性的、占优势的,支配的、统治的 [more dominant, most dominant]
④ **reality itself** 现实本身
⑤ **pixel** ['pɪksəl; -sel] *n.* (显示器或电视机图像的)像素

If you take a piece of something, you can break it down only to a certain size, now called "Planck's Length". (The size, in meters, is "1.6162 x 10 to the power of minus 35". Think of it as a **decimal**[1] point followed by 35 zeroes before you get to the actual numbers.)

These tiny elements of space make up reality in the same way that pixels make up the picture on your computer screen. It's a strange thought, isn't it?

Usually, it's good for students to listen to their teachers. But in this case, it was a good thing Max Planck didn't!

将一个物体进行分割，它分割成的可确定的最小尺寸，称为"普朗克长度"。（这个长度是 1.6162×10^{-35} 米，也就是说，它的小数点与后面的有效数字之间隔着 35 个 0。）

　　这种微小的基本元素构成了实体，就和电脑屏幕上像素构成了图像一样。这种想法很奇怪，是不是？

　　通常来说，学生听从老师的建议会受益匪浅，但对普朗克来说，幸好他没有听老师的话！

---

① **decimal** [ˈdesɪm(ə)l] *adj.* 小数的、十进位的；*n.* 小数

HOW A COMPASS INSPIRED A GENIUS

阿尔伯特·爱因斯坦
受到指南针启发的天才

ONE DAY, A DAD CALLED Hermann showed something to his little boy.

It was a compass. Compasses are interesting things. The needle moves around as you walk around. But it always ends up pointing in a certain direction. "It's showing us the way to the North Pole," Hermann said.

The little boy, whose name was Al, and who was about eight years old at the time, stared at the device in amazement.

Holding the compass in his hand, he turned himself in circles — but the needle always settled down to point in the same direction.

※※※

Most children are **intrigued**[1] the first time they see a compass, but soon forget it.

But not Al. He was a puzzle solver. We needed to know why it did, what it did. It was clear to him that some powerful invisible force existed in the world, and the compass was a clue to its existence. He determined to find out what it was and how it worked.

The boy, whose full name was Albert Einstein, soon took up a hobby of building mechanical things for fun.

But his father Hermann was not very successful with his electrical engineering business in his home country, Germany, so the whole family moved to Italy to find new customers. This was in the 1800s.

有一天，一位名叫赫尔曼（Hermann）的父亲给儿子看一样东西。

那是一个指南针。指南针很有趣，它的指针总是随着人的走动而改变方向，但停下后永远指向一个固定的方位。"它向我们指明了去北极的方向。"赫尔曼说。

他的儿子名叫艾尔，当时八岁。他盯着指南针，满脸惊奇。

他把指南针拿在手里，原地转圈——但指针最后总是指向同一个方位。

✦✦✦

大多数孩子第一次看到指南针时都会感到很好奇，但也很快就会忘了这件事。

但艾尔不一样，他热爱解密，喜欢探究事物的本质与缘由。他确信世界上存在一种看不见的强大的力，而指南针就是这种力存在的证明。他决定找到这种力，并探明它是如何起作用的。

不久，艾尔——他的全名叫阿尔伯特·爱因斯坦（Albert Einstein），有了一个爱好：造机械类物件，享受快乐心情。

但在 19 世纪，在他的祖国——德国，他父亲赫尔曼所经营的电气工程生意并不景气。为了开发新的客户，他们一家搬到了意大利。

---

① intrigue [ɪnˈtriːg] n. 阴谋、诡计、复杂的事、私通；vt. 用诡计取得，激起……的兴趣；vi. 私通、密谋 [intrigued，intrigued，intriguing]

When Al was about 14, he wrote a short **essay**[1] about science. It was called: "On the Investigation of the State of the **Ether**[2] in a Magnetic Field."

Clearly, magnetic power, like the force that moved compass needles, needed to move all the way from the North Pole to the compass in his Dad's hand. But how? Did it jump from **molecule**[3] to molecule?

No. Scientists already knew that magnetic forces could travel through a **vacuum**[4], which is a patch of emptiness containing nothing, no molecules, not even air.

At that time, 1894, people decided there must be an invisible substance in empty air. They called it "the ether". It had to exist to carry things such as magnetic forces and light particles.

But no one at the time ever found any of it.

Albert Einstein became very famous — one of the most famous scientists in history. He made his most important discoveries when he was a young man — with four discoveries in his 26th year alone.

He learned that the ether, as it was thought of in those days, did not exist. But there DID exist something called space-time, which we can think of as the basic "**stuff**[5]" of which reality is made. Some people think of space-time as a sort of "super ether".

❦❦❦

大约 14 岁时，艾尔写了一篇关于科学的短论文，题目是《磁场中以太状态之研究》。

显而易见的是，磁力，就是驱动指南针指针移动的力；需要从北极一直"移动"到他父亲赫尔曼手中的指南针上，但它是如何移动的呢？难道是从一个分子跳到另一个分子上的吗？

不。如今科学家已有结论，磁力能够在真空中传播，而所谓的真空，就是一个空无一物的空间，其中没有任何东西，连空气也没有。

那时，在 1894 年，人们认为真空中存在着一种不可见的物质，并将其称为"以太"。它的存在就是为了传播特定的物质，比如磁力和光的粒子。

但当时没有人发现过它。

❦❦❦

爱因斯坦声名鹊起——成了历史上最著名的科学家之一。当他还很年轻的时候，就作出了一生中最重大的发现——仅在 26 岁那年，他就作出了四项新发现。

他经过研究发现，当时人们所说的以太其实并不存在，但确实存在着"时空"这样的东西，我们可以将其视为构成现实的基础"物质"。有些人认为时空是一种"超级以太"。

----

① **essay** ['eseɪ] *n.* 散文，试图、随笔；*vt.* 尝试、对……做试验
② **ether** ['iːθə] *n.* 以太、苍天、乙醚
③ **molecule** ['mɒlɪkjuːl] *n.* 分子、微小颗粒、微粒
④ **vacuum** ['vækjʊəm] *n.* 真空、空间、真空吸尘器；[vacuums 或 vacua]
⑤ **stuff** [stʌf] *n.* 东西、材料、填充物，素材资料；*vt.* 塞满、填塞、让……吃饱；*vi.* 吃得过多

Other scientists have come to agree that the ether is actually a useful concept, although these days we use other names for it, such as "vacuum energy" or even "the **grid**[1]".

Einstein and Planck and their colleagues confirmed that even empty space is made of elements which can be thought of as pixels — little grainy pieces of reality: what an amazing thought!

当时其他的科学家都肯定以太实际上是一个有用的概念，尽管现在我们使用其他名字来称呼它，如"真空能"、"栅格"等。

爱因斯坦、普朗克和他们的同事证实，即使是空无一物的空间，也是由基本元素构成的，而这种元素可以视为类似于像素的颗粒状实体。这真是令人惊叹的发现啊！

---

① **grid** ［grɪd］*n*. 网格、格子、栅格、输电网

THE BOY SECRETLY READING A BOOK BEHIND HIS SCHOOL DESK

沃尔夫冈·泡利
在课桌下偷偷看书的男孩

TEACHER LOOKED AT HIS CLASS. As usual, some of the students were paying attention; some were not.

There was one boy in particular, whose name was Wolfgang, who seemed uninterested in what was being taught.

Instead, Wolfgang would sit with his head tilted forward. He was reading something he was holding behind his desk.

How did the teachers at school react to Wolfgang?

You'd think they would be angry, and probably some were, at first.

But in the end, Wolfgang didn't get into trouble. That's because the teachers discovered exactly what Wolfgang liked to read behind his desk. It was Albert Einstein's writings about **relativity**[1]!

These are a pair of scientific documents which are famous for being VERY difficult to understand.

It soon became clear that the reason why Wolfgang did not pay attention at school is that the lessons were far too easy for him.

He quickly understood what was being taught, and was hungry for more information, which he was finding himself.

❧☙

This scene, of Wolfgang reading in secret behind his desk, happened about 100 years ago in Germany. Einstein wrote about relativity in two works, one of which was published in 1905, and the other in 1916.

The boy, Wolfgang Pauli, read the works with great interest — even though they were so complicated that very few adults could understand what they were saying.

老师在课堂上环视一周,发现像往常一样,一些学生在认真听课,而另一些学生则在开小差。

有一个男孩表现特别。他名叫沃尔夫冈,似乎对课堂上的内容兴趣索然。

他坐在座位上,头微微前倾,正在看藏在课桌下的东西。

对此,学校的老师会有什么反应呢?

你可能认为他们会生气。确实,一开始时有些老师是挺生气的。

但在最后,沃尔夫冈并没有因此惹上什么麻烦。因为老师们发现,沃尔夫冈在课桌下偷看的,是爱因斯坦关于相对论的著作!

这是两篇以晦涩难懂而著称的科学文献。

很快老师就清楚了,沃尔夫冈上课不听讲,是因为这些课程对他来说太简单了!

他能够轻松地理解老师所教的内容,他渴求更多的知识,于是自己想办法去了解。

沃尔夫冈在课桌下偷偷看书这件事,发生在大约 100 年前的德国。爱因斯坦在两篇论文中提到了相对论,一篇发表于 1905 年,另一篇发表于 1916 年。

这些著作虽然晦涩难懂,能理解其意的成年人都寥寥无几,沃尔夫冈·泡利(Wolfgang Pauli)读起来却兴趣盎然。

① **relativity** [ˌreləˈtɪvɪti] n. 相对论、相关性、相对性

In these works, Einstein explained that reality was not what we thought it was. It could be thought of as a physical thing called space-time. And it could be shaped, or bent, or curved, by gravity. Even things that moved in straight lines, such as beams of light, could be shaped by gravity.

These were **stunning**① ideas, and Wolfgang was fascinated.

It turned out that the teachers were right to let Wolfgang do things in his own way.

The boy left school to go to university while still young, and finished his degree at the age of 18 (which is, of course, the age that most university students start their degrees).

Three years later, Wolfgang wrote an important work. Einstein himself wrote a note about it: "Whoever studies this **mature**② and **grandly**③ **conceived**④ work might not believe that its author is a 21-year-old man."

Wolfgang Pauli went on to become one of the most important scientists of the modern age. He worked on what are called the "fundamental particles" — this means the smallest pieces of matter, the little tiny things that make up everything in the world.

Even though these particles are too small to see, young scientist Pauli managed to deduce some important details about them, and is considered one of the fathers of quantum physics, the most **influential**⑤ set of findings in science in the past 100 years.

在这些著作中,爱因斯坦解释道,现实并不是我们所想的那样。我们可以把它看作是"时空"的物理存在,在万有引力影响下会变形、弯曲。即使是直线运动的物体,比如光束,在引力的影响下也可以改变形状。

这些观点令人震惊,沃尔夫冈被深深地吸引住了。事实证明,老师们允许沃尔夫冈以自己的方式进行学习是正确的。

沃尔夫冈十几岁时就进入了大学,18岁就完成了学业(大多数人在这个年纪才刚刚上大学)。

三年后,沃尔夫冈写了一篇重要的文章。爱因斯坦曾经这样写道:"任何阅读过这篇构思成熟作品的人都不会相信,它的作者竟然只有21岁。"

沃尔夫冈·泡利成了现代最重要的科学家之一。他致力于研究"基本粒子"——这是组成世间万物的最小粒子。

尽管这些粒子极其微小,根本看不见,但年轻的科学家泡利却设法推断出有关它们的一些重要信息,他因此被尊称为量子物理学创始人之一,而量子物理学是最近100年来科学界最具有影响力的发现。

---

① **stun** [stʌn] vt. 使震惊、打昏,给人以深刻的印象[stunned, stunned, stunning]
② **mature** [mə'tʃuə] adj. 成熟的、充分考虑的、到期的、成年人的;vi. 成熟、到期;vt. 使……成熟、使……长成、慎重作出[matured, matured, maturing, maturer, maturest]
③ **grandly** ['grændli] adv. 盛大地、宏伟地、堂皇地
④ **conceive** [kən'siːv] vt. 怀孕、构思,以为、持有;vi. 怀孕、设想,考虑[conceived, conceived, conceiving]
⑤ **influential** [ˌɪnfluˈenʃ(ə)l] adj. 有影响的、有势力的;n. 有影响力的人物

This does not mean that you, dear reader, should stop paying attention to your teachers and secretly read things behind your desk. (Unless, perhaps, it is science class and you are keeping your **enthusiasm**[1] high by reading this book!)

当然，亲爱的读者，这并不意味着上课时你就可以不听讲，在课桌下看自己的书了。(除非这是一堂科学课，而你正在看这本书，以保持自己对于科学的高度热情！)

① enthusiasm ［ɪnˈθjuːzɪæzəm］ n. 热心、热忱、热情

THE STUDENT WHOSE SCHOOLS KEPT CLOSING

李政道
学业一再中断的学生

IF YOU GET A DAY off school, you're pretty happy, right?

But what if you felt that you were born to be a science scholar but fate kept stopping you from going to school?

That was the problem of a boy called T.D. Lee, who loved books and learning.

Lee Tsung Dao lived in Shanghai when World War II **broke out**①. China was **invaded**② and his school was closed down.

So the boy who loved studying left school without any qualifications.

But luckily, he managed to pass the entrance examination of Zhejiang University.

Then his luck turned bad again. There was another invasion of China (the war was still continuing) and now his university was **forcibly**③ shut down!

Poor T.D. Lee. He must have felt that destiny was angry with him, which seemed unfair. He was a hardworking young student, and his family were good, well-respected people. (His grandfather was the rector of a very famous church in Suzhou.)

But it turned out that fate, secretly, had big plans for T.D. Lee. The **interruption**④ of his university studies meant that he had to move to Kunming, where he met a man called Professor Wu Ta-You, who **nominated**⑤ him for a Chinese government fellowship to study in the USA.

如果有一天不用上学,你会很开心,是不是?

如果你认为自己生来就注定会成为一名科学家,但命运却一再使你上不成学,你会怎么想?

这就是一个名叫李政道的男孩遇到的问题,他热爱读书、酷爱学习。

第二次世界大战爆发时,李政道居住在上海。中国遭受侵略后,他就读的学校被迫关闭了。

这位热爱学习的男孩只好离开学校,没有拿到任何资格证书。

✦✧✦✧✦

但幸运的是,后来他成功地考上了浙江大学。

接下来坏运气再一次降临。中国战火不断(第二次世界大战还在继续),浙江大学被迫停学!

可怜的李政道!他一定感觉到了,命运对他是如此的不公!他是个努力学习的学生,他的家人也都是善良而受人尊敬的人。(他的祖父是苏州一所著名教堂的牧师。)

但是命运似乎悄悄地在李政道身上实施着一个重大计划。大学学业中断意味着他必须去昆明(进入西南联大学习)。在那里,他遇到一位名叫吴大猷的教授。正是在吴教授的推荐下,李政道获得中国政府奖学金,得以赴美国留学。

---

① **break out** v. 爆发、突发
② **invade** [ɪnˈveɪd] vt. 侵略、侵袭、侵扰、涌入;vi. 侵略、侵入、侵袭、侵犯 [invaded, invaded, invading]
③ **forcibly** [ˈfɔːsɪblɪ] adv. 用力地、强制地,有说服力地
④ **interruption** [ˌɪntəˈrʌpʃn] n. 中断、干扰、中断之事
⑤ **nominate** [ˈnɒmɪneɪt] vt. 推荐、提名、任命、指定 [nominated, nominated, nominating]

In 1946, T.D. went to Chicago University and met a famous scientist, Professor Enrico Fermi, who noticed that the youngster was totally devoted to becoming a science **scholar**[①]. The Professor chose T.D. as a researcher.

Professor Fermi was one of the world leaders in modern physics. And that meant T.D. had a close-up view of the cutting-edge puzzles in science.

At that time, scientists had noticed an **intriguing**[②] phenomenon. When a person looks in the mirror, the image in the mirror is exactly the same as the real self, including appearances, dresses and movements. The same is true in the micro world. A fundamental particle is perfectly symmetric with its "mirror" particle. All the properties and motion are exactly the same.

This is the **Law of Parity Conservation**[③]. Scientists at the time thought the law was correct.

But some scientists have found that, in some cases, the motion of some particles does not fit the law.

After thorough researching work, T. D. Lee and a colleague, Yang Chen-ning, put forward their own theoretical **hypothesis**[④], boldly **asserting**[⑤] that parity is not conserved. They also proposed several experimental schemes. All the physicists were shocked.

He and his colleague C.N. Yang were given the Nobel Prize in 1957. T.D. was just 30 years old. (The woman who worked in the lab, running the experiments, also became famous — but that's another story which you can find in this book.)

1946 年，李政道进入芝加哥大学学习。在那里，他遇到了著名的科学家费米（Enrico Fermi）教授。费米教授注意到李政道想要成为一名科学家的决心，招收他做了自己的研究员。

费米教授是近代物理学的领军人物之一，这意味着李政道能够近距离地研究科学前沿问题。

那时，科学家注意到一个有趣的现象：当人照镜子时，镜中的影像和真实的自己完全一样——包括容貌、装扮和动作等。在微观世界里也如此，一个基本粒子与它的"镜像"粒子也完全对称，所有性质完全相同，运动规律也完全一致。

这就是"宇称守恒定律"，当时的科学家都认为这个定律是正确的。

但一些科学家发现，在某些情况下，有的粒子的运动不符合这个定律。

经过深入的研究，李政道和一位叫杨振宁的同事提出了他们自己的理论假说，大胆断言宇称不守恒，并提出了几种验证的实验方案。物理学家们大为震惊。

李政道和同事杨振宁在 1957 年获得了诺贝尔奖。当时李政道只有 30 岁。(那位在实验室中做验证实验的女子也因此出名——但那是另一则故事了，你可以在本书中读到她的故事。)

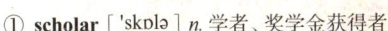

① scholar ['skɒlə] n. 学者、奖学金获得者
② intriguing [ɪnˈtriːɡɪŋ; ɪnˈtriːɡɪŋ] adj. 有趣的、迷人的；v. 引起……的兴趣
③ Law of Parity Conservation 宇称守恒定律
④ hypothesis [haɪˈpɒθɪsɪs] n. 假设 [hypotheses]
⑤ assert [əˈsɜːt] vt. 维护、坚持；断言；主张；声称 [asserted, asserted]

So the boy who thought that fate did not want him to be a science scholar ended up being **celebrated**① as one of the greatest science scholars of the century.

这位当初认为命运不想让自己成为科学家的男孩，最终还是成为这 100 年间最伟大的科学家之一。

---

① **celebrated** [ˈselɪbreɪtɪd] *adj.* 著名的、有名望的

THE BOY WHO HAD A DISPUTE WITH HIS FATHER

约翰·冯·诺伊曼
与父亲争论的男孩

ONCE THERE WAS A BOY called Jancsi who had an amazing ability to keep numbers in his head.

But his dad complained: "You'll never earn any money doing mathematics. You should be a businessman instead."

❦❦❦

You would not believe how good little Jancsi was when handling pages of numbers.

When guests came to the house of the von Neumann family, Jancsi's father, a banker named Max, would call his son to perform.

"Watch this," Max would say. He would open the telephone book at a **random**[1] page and hand it to his son. The child, who was just six years old, would read it.

Then the adults would pass around the book and read out names or addresses from that page.

Jancsi would tell them the **corresponding**[2] phone number, showing that he remembered everything on the whole page.

The boy could do **mental**[3] maths too, easily dividing pairs of eight-digit numbers in his head.

❦❦❦

The family lived in Budapest, Hungary, during the time of the First World War. They were Jewish, so life was dangerous.

But they survived the war, and when the boy was 15, a famous mathematician was brought to the house to give him extra lessons. The teacher was so astonished at the teenager's ability that he burst into tears, moved to be in the presence of a genius.

从前有个男孩叫扬奇（Jancsi），他有一种神奇的能力，能长久地记住数字。

但他的父亲对他抱怨道："你再怎么研究数学也是赚不到钱的，你应该去做一名商人！"

<hr />

你也永远想不到，年幼的扬奇多么擅长处理一页页的数字。

当有人来家里做客时，扬奇的银行家父亲马克斯·冯·诺伊曼（Max von Neumann）就会把儿子叫出来，让他展现自己的才能。

"看这个，"马克斯会说。他将电话号码簿随机翻到某一页，然后递给年仅六岁的扬奇看。

随后，马克斯和客人们传阅电话号码簿，念出上面的人名或地址。

扬奇则告诉他们与之对应的电话号码，表示他记住了电话号码簿上整页的内容。

扬奇也会心算，他能够在头脑中轻松地进行八位数的除法运算。

<hr />

第一次世界大战期间，扬奇一家住在匈牙利的布达佩斯。他们是犹太人，所以生命时刻处于危险之中。

所幸的是，他们安然度过了一战。当扬奇 15 岁时，一位著名的数学家成了他的老师，教授他额外的课程。扬奇的能力让这位数学家震惊不已，以致流下了激动的泪水。他认为扬奇是一位天才。

---

① **random** ['rændəm] *adj.* 随机的、任意的、胡乱的；*n.* 随意；*adv.* 胡乱地
② **corresponding** [ˌkɒrɪ'spɒndɪŋ] *adj.* 相当的、相应的、一致的，通信的
③ **mental** ['ment(ə)l] *adj.* 精神的、脑力的，疯的

But when it was time for Jancsi to go to university, the trouble started at home. He wanted to do a top university qualification, a PhD, in mathematics.

But his father wanted him to be a businessman. "There's no money in mathematics," he said. "Do something practical, like science."

What to do?

※

Jancsi himself came up with the answer. He **announced**[①] that he would sign up at two universities at once and do two degrees at once — one in mathematics, and one in chemistry.

And so he did.

His mathematics teacher at university was astonished at his student. Whenever he mentioned an unsolved problem in the world of calculations, the boy would immediately scribble down the answer.

These were not just test questions, but major problems that professional mathematicians were struggling with.

※

Well, in the long run, it turned out that Jancsi's father was wrong.

The boy, under his formal name of John von Neumann, became a super-famous mathematician.

And he did earn good money. In fact, he ended by sharing a university department with Albert Einstein, one of the smartest people ever.

然而，就在扬奇快上大学时，家中出现了一些问题。他想去一所顶尖的大学攻读数学博士学位。

但父亲要求他成为一名商人。"学数学将来赚不到钱，"父亲说，"你应该去学一些实用性的东西，比如科学。"

扬奇该何去何从？

❦❦❦

扬奇自己想出了答案。他宣布，自己将同时就读于两所大学，同时取得两个学位——一个数学、一个化学。

他确实做到了。

杨奇让他的大学数学老师震惊不已。无论老师在何时提出一个计算界尚未解决的问题，扬奇都能立刻不假思索地给出答案。

这些问题不是考试题，而是世界上专业的数学家们一直在努力攻克的重要难题。

❦❦❦

从长远来看，事实证明扬奇的父亲错了。

扬奇正式的名字叫做约翰·冯·诺伊曼（John von Neumann），他成了一位极负盛名的数学家。

他也赚到了一大笔钱。事实上，他后来与有史以来最聪明的人之一——爱因斯坦在同一所研究机构共事。

---

① announce [əˈnaʊns] vt. 宣布，述说，预示，播报；vi. 宣布参加竞选 [announced, announced, announcing]

John von Neumann's mathematics was so powerful that they needed it for quantum physics.

And when important new inventions were created, such as the atom bomb, scientists would call Jancsi (in the USA they called him "Johnny") to come and be in charge of the maths.

He was paid a lot of money. His dad should really have trusted him!

约翰·冯·诺伊曼的数学成就极具影响力，为量子物理学的发展作出了重要贡献。

每当人们开展重大的发明研究项目——比如研制原子弹时，科学家们都会请扬奇（在美国，人们称他为"强尼"）负责数学方面的研究。

这些研究也让扬奇得到了一大笔报酬。他的父亲本该相信，扬奇是能够赚大钱的！

The Young Scientists Series:
Fabulous Physics and The Amazing Quantum

by

Nury Vittachi

English Copyright © 2017 by World Scientific Publishing Co. Pte. Ltd.

Bi-lingual (Simplified Chinese & English) Character Copyright © 2018 by Shanghai Scientific & Technological Education Publishing House

Shanghai Scientific & Technological Education Publishing House published bi-lingual edition by arranged with World Scientific Publishing Co. Pte. Ltd., Singapore

All rights reserved. This book, or parts thereof, may not be reproduced in any form or by any means, electronic or mechanical, including photocopying, recording or any information storage and retrieval system now known or to be invented, without written permission from the Publisher.

ALL RIGHTS RESERVED

上海科技教育出版社业经World Scientific Publishing Co. Pte. Ltd.同意取得本书中英文双语版版权

| 责任编辑 | 侯慧菊 |
| 封面设计 | 杨　静 |

"伟人的少年故事"丛书
奇妙的物理学——推动物理学变革的惊世奇才
［斯里兰卡］努雷·维塔奇（Nury Vittachi） 著
斯泰帕·张（Step Cheung） 图
朱之翀　译
张　群　审校

出版发行	上海科技教育出版社有限公司
	（上海市柳州路218号　邮政编码200235）
网　址	www.ewen.co　www.sste.com
经　销	各地新华书店
印　刷	上海昌鑫龙印务有限公司
开　本	889×1194　1/32
印　张	3
版　次	2018年8月第1版
印　次	2018年8月第1次印刷
书　号	ISBN 978-7-5428-6710-0/G·3836
图　字	09-2017-937号
定　价	25.00元

扫描二维码
获取教师参考资料
及练习答案

扫描二维码
获取学生练习册